Performance-Based Certification